THE SINGING STONE

THE SINGING STONE

POEMS SELECTED BY
PAULINE STAINER

TO CELEBRATE
SIXTY YEARS OF THE
SUFFOLK POETRY SOCIETY

ORPHEAN PRESS
ON BEHALF OF
SUFFOLK POETRY SOCIETY
2012

First published in 2012
in a limited edition of 400 copies
on behalf of the Suffolk Poetry Society
by Orphean Press
10 Heath Close · Polstead Heath · Colchester CO6 5BE

No. 132 *of 400 copies*

Designed & typeset in ten- on twelve-point Berthold Caslon Book by
Peter Newble · 10 Heath Close · Polstead Heath · Colchester CO6 5BE
peter@newble.com · http://www.newble.com/

Printed and bound in Great Britain by Gipping Press
Unit 2 · Lion Barn Industrial Estate · Needham Market · IP6 8NZ

ISBN 978-1-908198-06-8

This anthology © 2012, Suffolk Poetry Society

British Library Cataloguing in Publication Data
A catalogue record for this book is available from the British Library.

CONTENTS

ACKNOWLEDGEMENTS

Most of the poems included in this anthology were award-winners in the Crabbe Memorial Poetry Competition and were first published by Suffolk Poetry Society. For the remainder the Society is grateful to those poets and their executors who have given permission for their work to be reproduced here. Strenuous efforts have been made to trace and contact the copyright holders of all works included, but for a small number the task has proved impossible. The Suffolk Poetry Society would be pleased to hear from any copyright holder whose permission has not been given, and to acknowledge them in future editions of this book.

Drawings by John Nash are reproduced by kind permission of the John Nash Estate.

THE FARMHOUSE WINDOW
Pen and ink drawing by John Nash, CBE, RA

INTRODUCTION

THE *Singing Stone* celebrates sixty years of the Suffolk Poetry Society. Most of these poems were award-winners in the annual Crabbe Memorial Poetry Competition. I have threaded them along the theme of an unfolding landscape, predominantly Suffolk, but with glimpses of more distant horizons. There are seascapes, woodlands, meadows, plough and furrow, saltmarsh, wilderness, edgeland. And journeys made by bicycle, road, train and on foot. All these poems are sharply observed, informed by history, tradition, those creatures which inhabit landscape, and the sacredness of the hearth. Ghosted airfields bear a freight of wild flowers; rock, gravel, water shift and are sifted. Poets are fired by a struggle between the inadequacy of language and the power of the word to illuminate. When the stone sings, landscapes become, indelibly, those of the heart.

PAULINE STAINER
President, Suffolk Poetry Society

LANDSCAPE, BOXFORD, SUFFOLK

ABOVE the village the ploughed ridges slope—
Brown earth air-softened as thrushes' feathers—
To a deckle of trees sewing a seam
Between fields, and drawing a line to mark
The underlying shape settled ages
Before these cultivations. Winter wheat shows
Its early green, and on clear days, in these
First months, there's a pastel light that shades where
Landscape folds fawn against blue, and distance
Sharpens the half-perceived familiar things.

The air makes moving invisible moulds
Over everywhere, slips through the furrows
And off the sides of saplings, and shivers
Through the green and tentative, pointing wheat;
And branches move within limits imposed
By growth. Birds court the currents, create, part
Them with briefly seen intentions. Hornpies
Especially carving aerobatic
Fretworks in flight. So always there is this
Imposition of ever-changing shapes.

These patterns, unseen, half-seen, have a kind
Of familiarity, or perhaps
A certainty contained by the land's fall;
Its own first shape that alone is seen, stays
Beneath the air-shapes, growth, and all that moves.
And standing here I would project on air
My own invisible cast among all
The others that have looked or worked, so this
Transience might become of the patterns,
A kind of ghost to be sensed in this land.

HARDIMAN SCOTT

INFINITE WHEELS

UNMOVING, you move through the mountains
of Wicklow still. Eyes closed to the coming
darkness, *the old haunts never more present.**
You propel your imagined wheels in unvarying
circles like the rims of Vico's history where
cycles of sufferings revolve like riddled leaves.

I see you pedal impassively along confined
roads across moors where dark pools reflect
altering sequences of cloud: the angular
spaces between pyramids of peat shot through
with pellets of sunlight, as the sea entices
in the smoked distance with its waves.

The tramps in your plays bear the imprints
of cycle clips long after they've lost their bikes:
they pine for their days of effortless motion:
happily downhill all the way with the scented
wind sifting their sparse locks of hair, beating
back the too solid air in their eternal figures of 8.

Like you, they long for the stillness
of cycling motion: that sensuous sail past
hedged fields where cattle revolve their jaws
on regurgitated grass. I see you again, on your
bed of death, raise your leaded right leg
to mount once more those infinite wheels.

JAMES KNOX WHITTET

* *In his last years, Beckett, when closing his eyes, was transported to the loved landscape he cycled through as a child.*

2

AN AMERICAN IN SUFFOLK

I T was you, John T. Appleby,
who led me to Chelsworth:
you, who spent just one summer
here in Suffolk, that of 1945;
you with your interest
in mediaeval churches
your passion for brasses;
your determination to be the last
American serviceman to leave.
You cycled all over the county
on a clapped-out machine
bought second-hand at a garage—
the kind of thing we treasured
then.

This was your favourite
village, and today the daffodils
outshine all your brasses. I
thank you for bringing me here,
you, who knelt so many hours
over likenesses of local gentry;
who almost became one yourself
before reluctantly taking your leave,
your bag crammed with delicate
silhouettes.

Now you are dead, I'd
like to think you have a real
brass of your own, that one day,
when these daffodils have bloomed
five hundred times, an Englishman
will copy, performing unconscious
homage on protesting knees.

FRANK WOOD

3

AIRFIELD, CASTLE CAMPS

SKYLARKS unreel their tinkling
ticker tape above the concrete
fractured street—a flight

off English ground, the green
silence, into the inhuman
vacancies—we live amongst

militant song, shrapnel
proliferates—nebulous
corals, nurses of flintstone

unfurl their barbarous flags,
projectiles seed the un-
appropriated air—the sea

whitens with dust, blackboard
chalk of a diagram in the
powdered skull of a Spitfire pilot.

CAMERON HAWKE SMITH

DUNKELD CATHEDRAL
Remembrance Sunday 2003

THE arrogance of men
who replaced the altar with a pulpit
turned ritual into performance
set words above music
above silence
exchanging mystery for matter

beyond the unroofed nave
and empty chancel
battalions of ancient larches stand
the hills the sun the clouds
an altar and incense
the valley of the Tay
His true cathedral

DAVID SIMPSON

4

A FLICKER OF BRACKEN

No more than a breath of wind against the field's skyline,
though there were so many other things I could have recalled,
like the colour of the house, the approach along the lane
where the hermit lived, the dropping of the cracked chamber pot on the flags
outside the kitchen so it couldn't mistakenly be used again,
the primroses on the bank and the bank of nettles separating
the garden from what we called the out there,
the adder country that was out there, the walk to the fallen tree, hornets
cruising from the bark that we prodded
quite childishly hard to break it up,
and the family of us, though I often pretended the family was something
I had simply come across.
            And the way
bracken twitched against the skyline, in a gap
between belts of pines, willing me to go on,
cross the field's plough and up to the edge,
as if there was something out there in the beyond
waiting for me to come to it. Once, before the light had properly
stroked the land awake I found this tunnel of mist leading to trees on the horizon,
wisps of white air breaking up half way across broken ground,
like a secret not to be shared
as I ran forward, forward with my arms outstretched to receive.

ROBIN MAUNSELL

THE HARE

HARE in the field opposite;
Lying stone flat in the clay earth.
Still, watchful, patient for the dusk.

Pert winter corn,
Bristles on a brush,
Marks out his distance from the hedge.

The loping ears,
The deep brown eyes,
Give him thirty yards start on anything.

Rain and chill autumn frost,
Temper the muscle.
His coat steams lazily at mid-day.

His time is organised
for patient survival
Waiting for the crocus.

GERARD MELIA

PRECOCIOUS PERSEPHONE

PERSEPHONE, it's far too soon for spring.
Earth is bereaved. Give her some time to mourn
the year that died a week or two ago.
Stop daubing colours on the countryside
with such infectious speed and disrespect.
That gaudy orange on the poplar's twigs,
and hedgerow bushes burning red,
viridian shoots of Queen Anne's Lace that itch
their way up through the moist soil unopposed,
it is too soon for them.
Let them alone!

And tell the open catkins to recoil,
and save their pollen for a warmer time.
Send back the wind to true and honest north
with fierce blue skies or monumental clouds.
It should be boreal in January.
Persephone, if you must have the sun,
then let it shine on convalescent fields
of muted browns and greys, not blazing green.
You left the underworld impulsively.
Return there for a while,
while earth revives.

The pure sharp anonymity of snow,
revealing tracks of animals and birds,
or narrow bodkin-eyes of snowdrop buds
which thread their way through matted meadow grass.
To you, the simple comforts that I draw
from Nature's reticence are alien.
Persephone, am I too hard on you?
For ignorance of winter is no fault
when it is something you can never see
or breathe or hear or touch.
How much you miss!

DIANA HIRST

CONTEMPLATION

I LEANT on Dunnottar Castle's field-stile
Lingering by the ruin's entrance
Watching fat sheep on green hillocks
Waddle
Ther fluffing woollen fleeces
Swinging
Like greatcoats in the wind
This way
That way
Shifting their heaviness
Behind the gusting air
Carrying their unborn lambs
A caravan of innocents
Preparing for the birth journey
And I think of Prestonpans
As Jonnie Cope's man
Slept
While Charlie's boys
Crept in for the slaughter

PENNY HEMANS

AIRD MOR

At the back of a cave discreetly screened
by a curtain of watery lace
a hind lies on her side, legs stiff
with blackened tongue and vacant eye.

Beneath her tail in vain protrude
two perfect, pointed, cloven hooves.

She should have torn his caul away,
licked clean his nostrils, eyes and mouth
and nudged at him to stand then felt
the triumph of first milk, his greed
as gums clamped onto brimming teats.

She should have led him through wet drapes
into the sun, the glittering. The shush and pull
of heaving sea, the piping cry
of Bridget's birds; and shown him how
to tread his way on shingle shore and shale
between the cliff and twisting waves.

Whose heart stopped first? Her unborn fawn?
Or did the hind give up the fight,
while he still struggled to reach the light?

The pain—rolling in waves—subsides.
Blinds draw down over her eyes.
The plashing of water fades and dies.

ANNE BOILEAU

FEN FLOOD

THAT night the sea rose up and rinsed
the edges of the Wash,
crept over peat and marsh,
breached the Earl of Bedford's dikes,
burst Denver sluice and Earith lock,
swamped bushes, alder, age split willow,
slunk into homes and farms and barns,
tugged boats from moorings, tractors from sheds,
drowned Domesday villages, Stuntney, Haddenham,
then swallowed Ely's isle to lap
at the great cathedral door.

As word got round in the blackness of night,
it laughed at the pitching and shoving of men
poured into this so-called Ship of the Fens,
a second arc which would not float.
Nothing survived, no mammals, fish or fowl,
except a couple of elver eels who lived to breed again.

ANGELA PICKERING

TIDESCAPE

SOMETIMES high tides invade salt-marshes here,
Slide in quiet channels between samphire and sea-lavender,
Then, pre-ordained, retreat, moon-dragged
To thin scribble on sky's rim.

It is not often though that sea is winched so far,
Beyond sight, as it is today; not often its bleak
Hinterland is so extended. I walk,
Curious, charting a new country.

First, sand, rippled with shallow lapping,
Pocked with shells and little stones; then
Like wings, smooth banks carved and curved
Round pools and still-running streams.

After these, far out, a strange other world,
A lonely planet, sculpted, silent, stark,
In surreal light; not chasm-split or heaved
In peaks, but more sinisterly

Gouged and scooped, worn with whirlpools, spun
And sucked with currents, subtly marked with violence.
It is as well concealing layers are seldom stripped
This far. We are not anxious to have such scars exposed.

MARY MARKWELL

FLINTS

SHINGLE clothes this shore-line
like a Joseph's coat,
spectrum of brown, dun, ochre,
beige and ivory
mottled with other hues,
but each pebble sleeked by waves
to uniform shape of orb, egg or disc,
disciplined and rounded to anonymity
by the sea.

Not so the eccentrics, those knubbly flints.
Their quirky rough-hewn lumps are
instantly recognised
though no two the same.
Like ancient schoolmasters they wear
dusty old coats worn thin
and frequently discoloured,
white chalk yellowing with age.
The sea has scrubbed their skins
but cannot hide their crankiness;
irregular and tactile they resemble
knuckle-joints or ham bones,
a clenched fist, club foot or bull's head.

Split them open and their startled, exposed faces
gleam with the beauty of a starling's wing.

MARY HODGSON

THE SINGING STONE
for Helen

SHORE-walking, heron-hunched, so long now;
the youngest reckoned, at first, it was about

filling my coat with grasps of sea grit, weed
and pebble; until they found a sailor's pearl,

a fairy shield, could tell a cowrie from a unicorn
and flint charms, which the sea, for good luck

had softened and sucked its way clean through.
This late winter brings a singing stone

from under the storm down Dunwich way;
a squat grail, half-tunnelled, whose secret eye

sings to my second breath, a frail note
of elfin song, higher than wash of waves;

like instant silver, drawn from its dull ore
gleaming sea-bright in the falling shade.

MIKE BANNISTER

TILLEY FISHERS
AT SOUTHWOLD

OCTOBER. A night
too bright to stay indoors;

we look down from the cliff path
see coloured umbrellas
wedged low in shingle,
tilted to shield men
and tilley lamps
on this windy coast.

Their outline blurred,
lit from within,
the colours flame the beach
like magic mushroom caps.
They drug the eye,
cannot be caught on camera.

Fishermen
when shoals come inshore
stake out rods,
lamp, cooking fire, umbrella,
create a myriad glow-worms, bait
fed on fantasy.

Waves gleam silver,
full moon highlights
like fishscales
on the water
diminish to meet the horizon,
moving stones are outlined
as boots crunch in shingle banks.

Breakwaters walk black
step by step into the sea
to where waves break
white in the dark.

Each fishing group
is as tight as a family.
In the air hangs a scent
of driftwood burning.

Every Autumn
there is the same
concentration
on fish that never fail to come.

In Summer
visitors
catch never a one!

MARGUERITE WOOD

LOBSTER FISHING
AT DAWN

COBBLES stretch like a street
of huge black pearls,
children step to the boat,
smell salt and rope,
raw fish.

The sea has drowned
some stars,
it seems the Lady of Waves
will raise
an enchanted sword
within the harbour walls.

They are aware
of shabby paintwork,
scuffed wood,
but this is the ship that flew,
the crew are safe
in chainmail knitted in rib,
each boathook
carries the sun on its tip
like a lance.

They see no mermaid hair
or serpent slain,
but those gigantic claws
in pots might
haunt a crack in some
sea-hall and
nightly walk its floor.

ISOBEL THRILLING

LOCKE'S ORCHARD

A TOWER of light with a bright pin fixes
apple leaves, like a collage of moths
and I can see the tree stepping from its rich
greens as a swimmer slips out of his clothes

or rises from a pool, splitting its ripe
skin and trailing strings of joyful beads.
The world lies naked as a new born child
to those with tutored eyes to guide their heads.

But we are locked away from its cropped glare
and see the world's flat ghost as through a glass;
our mind the hawk perched on a pin of air,
the waiting worm curled at the apple's heart.

ROSS COGAN

JEWELS

HALF in the lake I pause and stand.
I may not move to launch away,
But in the shallows stare and stay
Between the water and the land.

Here, where the floating lily lies,
Where grasses bend above the pool,
The air is lustrous with the cool
Fragility of dragonflies,

As one by one or two by two
They hover in a slender sheen,
Green in a subtlety of green,
Blue as the pure idea of blue.

They hand and flit or stud a reed
In jade or azure parallels,
The straight bodied desmoiselles
That end so lissomly at need;

The live yet lapidary things
With dip and turn and sway and lift,
Darting or posed upon the swift
Invisibility of wings.

And here I stay and watch alone.
Alone? Or could they strangely tell,
These that love and know so well,
They are more loved and better known?

That, where the sun-shot alders lean,
Some jeweller angel of this place
Makes as a portrait of a Face
This live yet lapidary scene:

A figure cut in ivory
Set in a moonstone, lapped with light;
And, hung on blades of malachite,
Brooches of lapis lazuli?

FRANCIS ENGLEHEART

MEMORY OF DEBACH, 1955

A BLURRED recall of summer, naïve, rough-edged,
Almost a woodblock print from Chaucer's world:
The hidden boy sits high in a greengage tree,
An ancient Suffolk countryman walks by.

Life's paintbrush wants to tint this Book of Hours,
To animate the imp among the peeping leaves,
Where droning wasps seek silence at the plummy ooze
Above old Hubbard's wheezing, timeless gait.

He's walked this path for several hundred years,
His ancient gaberdine is rank with slops
From buckets for the sow behind the blackthorn hedge.
Likewise the changeless child forever grips

The branch, wide-eyed and queasy at the reek
of swill that mingles with the heavy bloom of fruit.
The mind must strive to make that past agree with now,
But muscle knows the reach of every greengage bough.

KEITH ROSE

FRIDAY-STREET FARM-SHOP

TODAY we are shopping for words:
succulent but tart,
or sweet and juicy when squeezed;
press your ears gently into the end of 'melon'.

Long fat words, like 'asparagus'
or 'cucumber'—that dark green grin—
or 'bananas' spraying from their stem
like the opening burst of a Sten gun:
'ba-na-na-na-na-nas'.

Short round plump ones:
'plums' and 'peas' and 'grapes'.
Relish the sound of 'radish' in your mouth;
try 'baby beet'. or sink your ears
into a crunchy 'Cox's Orange Pippin'.

How exotic the sounds of 'mango',
'litchi', paw-paw' taste. How
pungent 'okra', 'garlic', 'quince' and 'kumquat'.
Be seduced by the fruitiness
of 'nectarine' and 'canteloupe'.

Play happy famiies with the sounds
of 'kale', 'Kohl rabi', 'broccoli',
'cauliflower', 'coleslaw', calabrese'.
'Potatoes and 'tomatoes' are related.

Words we've hardly noticed, all this year,
perk up like wilted lettuce in iced water.

ROY BLACKMAN

SUNDAY NIGHT

THE partings are final,
Railway stations are specially designed
For momentary heartbeat.

No car door will slam
Hurried steps, an apologetic knock
And, 'I've left my gloves'.

But instead down the platform
Loaded with mail-bags and strange slatted crates,
A whistle blows.

And wailing, somehow embarrassed minds
Suddenly search for one complete, overwhelming word,
Which never comes.

In its place comes the inadequate:
'See you next week', or even just:
'Goodbye'.

And when the train has slid into the dark
Some turn, or shrug with duty done,
Or pat a patient dog.

But some, the young, the untaught, stand naked,
Each crudely bisected from the one person who can
Make the face smile again.

DAVID L. JOHNSON

OWLS

Tonight,
the moon is a river.
A silver shadow whose face we admire.
The moon turns the river's pages
like a book.
Softly, the pages turn, one by one.
In the river ourselves, our faces, turning.
Here where the edges of trees frisk our shadows
and trace the night shapes of houses—
we are watching for owls.
I am convinced they are near.

It is only that the dark trees are hiding them.
It is only that the old boats are hiding them.
The owls fly inside my own eyes—in and in,
flying lower and lower. My thoughts become feathers.
My dreams have no edges. Flight swallows me.
I am owl and moon and river and night.
The stars watch over me—the pulse of water
greets me, keens for me
that I must watch here, so late. It is the hour for owls.
I hear the slow beating of their coming.
A train passes, holds the moon in each of its windows.
Myself, I am held by the promise of owls.
My throat holds a shadow, it grows and grows
and from it
flies the first of them.

HELEN BURKE

A HEDGE DESTROYED

Soon you will forget
How traveller's joy, roses and may
Lined this part of the way,
A barricade thick and rich
As that which twined and crept
Upwards for a hundred years
While a girl waited and slept—

But when snow comes
Sifting thinly across,
You may remember
How somewhere here
The road used to seem kinder,
And a bird heading home
When the loaded truck was gone,
Hovered, baffled by the space,
Before flying on.

JENNIFER ANDREWS

THE NEW WASTELAND

Look at the hedges where you pass—
Into the ditches strewn with broken glass;
Onto the trampled roadside grass

Covered with paper wrappings, tins;
A sea of waste around the litter bins,
Churned by the probing, seeking winds.

Stop where the wayside spinney's dip
Slopes to a straggling, tangled rubbish tip,
The scene of nature's failing grip.

Follow the new road's scything gash
Over the stumps of oak, beech, elm and ash;
Constructed so that men may dash

Through a new landscape flattened out
From the old, the twisting, the roundabout;
Having never the slightest doubt

The quickest route is always the best . . .
Why do we never pause for peace or rest?
Why this mania within the breast?

Even the fields bear folly's crop—
Birds, insects, flowers, reptiles and mammals drop
Dead on the hardened altar top

Of desiccate, spray-poisoned earth.
While overhead, sprung from a foreign birth,
Steel pylons belt the country's girth.

And in the distance, seen to rise,
Dark castellations lowering at the skies,
Clouding with smoke our searching eyes.

A blot has stained our rural page.
How can we break the iron of the cage?
Are we but products of the age?

D. R. Butcher

WORN DOWN

Low lane, deep lane
where the carts and horses came
between blackthorn, hips and haws,
down to the barn and then the farm.
For years of hard lives.

Cold wind, wet ground
where the turnips were wrenched out
to feed the sheep. The hips proclaim
Winter's walls will tumble down
letting in the colour of Spring.

Must, dust and sweet hay,
in the barn where they were throwing
food for the cows into a cart,
backed through the wide doors;
while the owl peered down.

Green ground, brown ground,
a lawn where there was corn,
corduroy where there was none.
Their lives might seem monotonous
but many of them loved the land.

Corn was sown by none of note;
long gone: skilled men.
We have inherited their land
and I hope their care of it:
but now it has no green plover.

Strong kings, weak kings,
still the ploughmen cursed the weather;
and cut the corn, and named the flowers,
lords-and-ladies, love-in-the-mist,
sleeping beauty, cuckoo flower.

Black trees, brown bracken
in a month this lane will be
gleaming with celandines. Lit
with stitchwort: loud with lark,
foaming with blackthorn blossom.

GILLIAN BENCE-JONES

HOUSE POND IN
HIGH MIDWINTER

A WIDE bowl flanged with
Slabbed mud; soft trodden cobbles
Of glossy ooze dotted
With little sky blue mirrors.
Dim at the margin,
Marbling slow boiled clouds
Of pumped silty drifts.
Hoofs chop the soft crust,
Paddle prints in frilled clods
Upturned on the black and green rim.

White for so long; white glazed
Like a cool gritty porcelain
Snowed over.
Dead shreds of grass
Hang in crisped silks,
Dry and straw coloured
Till weak sunlight fires
Golden lustres.
Deft calligraphies
Laquer the snow bowl.

Under bright moonlight
Ice tightens and sighs,
Settles a shoulder back under
The fallen blanket of snow;
Dreams the tense weight
Of a white horse stepping.
Sniffing frost. Again stepping.
Cautious, the whiskered head looms.
Nostrils plume his own ghost in mist,
Till, at the centre,
He pauses, still, under moonlight;
Floats frozen hooves over land
He knows never was there.

Two months under.
Blackly the drugged pond slept
Under a thick lid of ice.
We beat at it with metal gate bars
Till a thin trickle seeped
From fractures chipped at the edge;
Cold clear water coaxed
From its frozen coma.
The white horse still waits,
Shouldering wind from the North.

KIM BAKER

HORSE SENSE

TETHERED to a rail post in the stable yard, Sparkle,
fidgety as a dental patient, awaits the farrier.
New shoes to be fitted, hooves cleaned, a pedicure.
These days the mountain comes to Mohammed.
The Smith is familiar, but his mobile forge
hisses and rumbles with appalling menace.
Ears swivelling and eyes rolling, Sparkle snickers
half in fright, dances with nervous anticipation.
Speaking softly he strokes the horse's muzzle
then gently runs his hands down each leg.
The Smith's voice is a constant ululation, a lullaby,
soothing sound as he works his way round the feet.
Firmly lifting each leg in turn to quickly remove
the worn shoe, clean and file each hoof.
The voice unwavering, encouraging, a love song
to the anxious horse. The work goes smoothly on.
One remains, the nearside rear and then the job is done.
The horse becomes impatient and starts to snort.
Old Gambit, watching over his stable door, whinnies.
Sparkle, distracted, snuffles and the work is finished.
One closing check, then the horse is walked,
a precocious model round a cobbled catwalk.
A final word, a pull on the ears, a kiss on the muzzle.
'You'll do for me, lad.' The Smith departs.

TERRY BUTLER

LOGGING

My grandson comes with me today, as I
go up into the wood for logs.
He rides inside my barrow as it jogs
across the meadow, full of questions:'Why

do cats and foxes come out in the night?'
'Will there be bears in there?' and 'Could your axe
chop wolves in half?' He squats upon the sacks,
avoids my lurking bow-saw and holds tight.

There in the coppice, I cut up my wood
happy to show him how I lift and swing
the cords in place, telling him where to bring
the fallen-off cuts. He has understood

exactly my procedure, fills up the bags
and balances the barrow with its load.
And then I see him in the narrow road
dragging a length of hornbeam: one end sags

along the muddy rut, the other's nipped
beneath his arm. 'This next,' I hear him say.
Then I perceive, not far off now, the day
when his hold will have tightened, and mine slipped.

JOHN WATTS

HAZEL

THE Suffolk lane unwinds, shining winter-wet,
sprinkled with fine twigs,
bordered with mud seeping off carved clay fields.

Tall trees scrape the buttery sky
and hold the last of the sun in their bare branches.

The telegraph poles
count out the distance we have travelled,
their loping wires moaning a sad Siberian tune.

I am taking a man I have known all my life
away from his dying wife to a lonely house

where she used to preside unobtrusively
over the teapot, the immaculate tablecloth
laden with her sweetness, the buns
glistening with chocolate icing,
the perfect shortbread.

As a treat she would unveil
the mechanical bird,
that cocked its head,
dabbed its tail,
calling across two centuries
with its vibrant tune.

The cage is covered now.

FLORENCE COX

BLYTHBURGH
CHURCH BIRDS

ENTER, but the notice says,
close the wire screen door
to keep the birds out please
otherwise
they will fly in and die.

Step inside the church.
It's a cage of light falling on stone.
A movement above,
steady now

a horde of Hitchcock beating wings,
squadrons of angelic harriers
coming at you,
flying high above the runway nave.
The whistle of feathers straining air.

Shut that church door quick,
don't let those angels out
beyond their rafters, pillars,
they'll spread too strong a song outside,
raise havoc
over pigs and cars,
river, marsh,
dirt-track bikes.
Turn our world
inside out.

JUDITH CRAMOND

PEACOCKS IN POLSTEAD

THERE'S a bend in the road
where I sometimes see peacocks.

This is Suffolk—
pink-washed houses,
tidy lawns,
cherries at the gates
for sale, and fields beyond
of ripening corn,
a little copse, a lane, and then
suddenly,
there they come;
tiptoe, pecking 'cross the road,
nodding heads of feather crests,
carrying extra eyes behind,
cushioned in gold and turquoise blue,
waiting for weddings to open out
and strut their stuff for dowdy brides.

As suddenly, they're gone.

But I'm left dreaming of processions;
pipes and drums that wail and clang;
dancing girls with bangles tinkling,
stamping feet with ankle bells.

Jasmine thrown by jewelled hands.

A tusker follows—high aloft
the maharajah, silken turbaned,
swaying, regal, left and right—
fills the road and turning, changes

into a tractor—growl and grind.

The passing driver lifts his hand
in very English wave of thanks,
and I drive on to games of cards
and cardboard kings
in games of bridge.

WENDY PARTRIDGE

THE SCARECROWS

HERE cometh the scarecrows.

They drift in from lonely farmsteads
tired of drunken farmers
the relentlessness of the weather
the high spirits of country children

exhausted by crows

they gather on the lawns of the mansion
a quiet assembly of the meek and forsaken.
Some have managed bicycles
others are foot weary
exasperated by wing feathers

without ale.

Many lie on the grass like trench soldiers
pleased at the discovery.
Others affect a dandyish air with yellow cloth
sharpening their hedge-torn coats.

They do not ask for charity.

The townsfolk bring their children
so they can see the difference.
The children ask ' Why don't they speak?'
The parents say 'Because they are dumb.'
The children think 'What difference?!'

This year conkers are many.

The wind is a little fresher
the Indian summer is fading,
leaves are more down than up.
The scarecrows have decided to go
leaving no litter, no forwarding address.

JULIAN STANNARD

THE WILD SWANS AT ALDEBURGH

SOME days they look like outsize geese
with no secret, seen
waddling across reclaimed land
to a ditch. Thirteen:
my lucky number. But one, hatched out too late,
is without a mate.

The trees are in their winter grandeur.
A line of pine trees stands
aware of me as I of them—
children holding hands.
We watch a ditch ruffle like elephant skin
and the sun whiten and thin.

I track a curlew in a cloud
by its call: fast headway.
The thirteenth swan has taken off:
an immature grey,
it creaks a low flight, then stands and walks alone,
feeling its half-soul gone.

Pathetic these fallacies our lives fatten.
Forty years are lost
since I first read Yeats, yet never see
a swan without his ghost.
A swan in death and I in life both read
the bobbin, rewinding the thread.

December sunshine brings white joy,
a milky hole in light.
These weeks three friends or almost-friends
have taken that silver flight
to some new pond or ditch or reclaimed land.
As souls, or swans, we stand

in a place of no giving in marriage.
Aware or unaware,
a leap through inarticulate light
defines some strangled prayer,
leaving us stripped, deciduous winter trees,
hand in hand, or on our knees.

HERBERT LOMAS

34

ASH
for my father

MORNINGS like this, before the haze lifted
you'd have swum with the sunrise, breakfasted well,
been first even then to the boatyard, pushing off
your Loch Long from the slipway, carried out
past the anchored patricians, through Tempests and Dragons,
their tap-tapping halyards applauding your gliding,
that water-slap salt-muddy tang as your featherlight cradle
tacked by in a flapping of canvas, set its downriver course
for Blackstakes and Orford and sight of the sea, surrendered
to gusts that tugged at your dandelion wisps, your brick-red
windbreaker cheeks that beamed in that solitary bliss

and again now you drift
from my grasp, sift from the clench of my palm
in this cool early mist to re-enter the shallows,
the last pale semblance of you, shimmering afloat
on the slipway, light as blown dandelion still, at play
like a shoal clinging yet to itself, still somehow
a body, this albescent glow moving under the surface,
shining back its own ghost-light, some mysterious
new being settling into your element, pausing
here in the lap of clear water—
luminous, swaying, slowly deeper and out—
weightless, ashimmer, released.

ANDRÉ MANGEOT

AFTERWORD

SUFFOLK Poetry Society is celebrating its very own Diamond Jubilee in step with the Queen. Our Society represents another more modest strand of continuity through the shifting life of our nation. Reading these poems, which are predominantly but not exclusively about Suffolk, I am reminded of the peculiar beauty of this county.

I was born in Boxford—it is quite by chance that the first poem in this book is a tribute to that village—'distance sharpens the half-perceived familiar things' (page 1)—but when I was seven we moved up north to Nottinghamshire, where the air was full of smuts and the landscape blighted by industrial pollution. So, like Beckett, who cycled in his mind through his native Ireland, I looked back on Suffolk as a kind of paradise—a place of 'pink-washed houses, tidy lawns' (page 32) of 'low lane, deep lane' (page 25) where 'cobbles stretch like a street' (page 16) and our 'boots crunch on shingle banks' (page 14). I remembered the barn owls in our barn; paddling with my brother in the Box, boating on Thorpeness Meare; I saw the 'fragility of dragon-flies' (page 18) and watched 'a swan without his ghost' (page 34). And, because we lived so far inland, I longed for the 'tides' and 'salt-marshes' (page 11).

I feel greatly privileged to be part of this landmark in the life of Suffolk Poetry Society. Our members, both living and dead, are united in a fellowship of poetry and place. We know our way around the twisting lanes; we share a familiarity with and affection for the same villages and towns whose names call up shared images in our mind: Polstead, Southwold, Chelsworth, Aldeburgh; Haddenham, Blyth-burgh, Orford. And let's not forget the gentle rivers: Brett, Lark, Blyth, Stour, Waveney, Orwell, Ouse, *etc.* Our magazine is now named after them: *Twelve Rivers*; they flow slow and clear as they always have and always will, just like the river of poetry.

ANNE BOILEAU
Chairman. Suffolk Poetry Society
July 2012

SUFFOLK POETRY SOCIETY
1952–2012
MORE THAN A 'PARNASSIAN MOLEHILL'

Ask many people to describe Suffolk in three words and the responses are likely to include 'farming', 'fishing', and 'flat'. Farming and fishing have engaged Suffolk families for centuries. Both involve hard toil and danger. Most of the workers were never able to lift themselves above the breadline. Yet it is in these situations that community thrives. People get together to play instruments, to tell stories, to sing or even to write poetry.

But is Suffolk flat? The Earl of Cranbrook compiled an anthology referring to Suffolk, called *Parnassian Molehill*. Mount Parnassus in Greece is over 8,000 feet tall and is home to the Greek Muses, whereas Suffolk's tallest point is Great Wood Hill at only 420 feet. The point the Earl makes is that the Muse lives just as much in Suffolk as Parnassus. Even so, Suffolk is not flat. Suffolk undulates beautifully within her 420 feet to produce lovely rolling hills and vales.

So what stirs a poet's heart and makes him or her write passionately? Yes, it is this hardship, reversal of fortune, the rolling land, the raging seas and the mackerel skies, but it is also the people around us, our loved ones, our foes, our innermost thoughts and feelings and, of course, other poets.

Suffolk is blessed with an outstanding poetic tradition and it deserves to be studied in an effort to enhance each individual poet's work. Realising this, in May 1928 a group of individuals—Herbert Hudson, Joan Hudson and Francis Engleheart—got together to form the Suffolk Poetry Club. They read and sent their own poems to one another for criticism by means of what is nowadays called a portfolio, they held public recitals, and they arranged for eminent poets and scholars to visit the club to read. They also ran themed meetings at which members would read their own poems on a particular subject. The Club continued until 1939 when war was declared, and was then disbanded until things had settled down. In 1952 Francis and Joan re-formed the old Club and called it the Suffolk Poetry Society. They had seventy attendees at their first meeting and fifty immediately signed up for membership. The aims and purpose of the Society were very much as before. Meetings were held, lectures given, people read their own poetry, public recitals were given and, in 1955, a portfolio was re-introduced. The themed aspect of writing poems, even for the Crabbe Memorial Poetry Competition, continued well into the 1970s.

You might ask: what is the Crabbe Memorial Poetry Competition? When the Earl of Stradbroke, who was also Lord Lieutenant of Suffolk, realised that 1954 was the 200th anniversary of the birth of the poet George Crabbe in Aldeburgh, a sub-committee of the Society was formed to introduce the Crabbe Memorial Poetry Competition. It was a very weighty committee in that it included two earls and two knights. It raised £300 to fund the competition and had a rose bowl made for the winner.

In 1955 the first winner of the Crabbe, as it is often referred to, was Alfred Ernest Tomlinson, for a poem entitled 'Suffolk Sky'. A well-known anti-war poet, in 1913 in Cambridge he had gained notoriety and publicity for a public disagreement with Rupert Brooke, though otherwise he was a very private sub-postmaster in Lowestoft.

Early in the Society's history a member, now unknown, donated a statue of George Crabbe, believed to have been sculpted *circa* 1848 by Thomas Thurlow of Saxmundham. This statue used to be carried in procession into the prize-giving ceremony; this became quite a tradition. It was then loaned to the Ipswich Museum and the ceremony came to an end. At present the statue is in the Moot Hall Museum in Aldeburgh.

The Crabbe is among the longest-running provincial poetry competitions in the country. The first prize has been won four times each by Gillian Edwards and James Knox Whittet. Julian Stannard won three times in a row and in 1974 Marguerite Wood was awarded both joint first prizes. Among the Crabbe's better known adjudicators have been Sir Charles Tennyson, John Betjeman, Philip Larkin, Frances Cornford and Thomas Moult. Recently they have included the former Poet Laureate, Andrew Motion, and George Szirtes.

In its archives the Society has newsletters and minutes of annual general meetings and committee meetings going back to the 1980s, and has recently recovered a full set of the winning Crabbe poems, not only for its records but so that those interested can research them. Maintaining an archive is just one way in which the Society shows its dedication to learning.

The Society continues to innovate with events such as readings at the Bury Festival (the 'Desert Island Poems') and vocal coaching. Increasingly the Society and the Café Poets groups have arranged for members to visit other groups and provide readings. Another major undertaking in the last ten years was the production of combined music and poetry events called 'Schubertiads'.

A lot of good work is undertaken on Suffolk dialect and on translating important poetry from other languages. A visit to the Sutton Hoo Anglo-Saxon burial site resulted in translations and readings from Old English and, importantly, it provided new subject matter for members to write about in an informed way.

Some members benefit from weekend breaks when they can focus on certain aspects of their poetry. The 2011 weekend in Othona, near Bradwell, was so popular it is being repeated with a different theme.

It is often said that if you captivate a person's mind while still a child, you will sow seeds that the child can reap throughout life. It is important for any society to attract new members and many of them will have developed a love of poetry when they were children. It is for this reason that the Society created the Hardiman Scott Award, a children's poetry competition in memory of a past President, Hardiman Scott, known to us as Peter.

All these activities and events take us back to the start of this essay: observing the world around us, getting in touch with our true thoughts and feelings and using the poetry of others to spur us on. Poetry in Suffolk is alive. Long may the Muses sing in what is more than just a 'Parnassian molehill'!

ROD O'DONOGHUE
Archivist, Suffolk Poetry Society

PRESIDENTS		CHAIRMEN	
Sir Francis Meynell	1952–1967	Francis Engleheart	1952–1963
Ralph Nixon Currey	1968–1979	Eric Sandon	1963–1971
Hardiman Scott, OBE	1979–1999	Romilly Redfern	1971–1976
Herbert Lomas	1999–2008	Marguerite Wood	1976–1988
Mike Bannister	2009–2010	Catherine Dell	1988–1997
Pauline Stainer	2010–	Mike Bannister	1997–2002
		Ionne Hammond	2002
		Beryl Sabel	2002–2007
		Frank Wood	2007
		Gerard Melia	2008
		Fred Ellis	2008–2011
		Anne Boileau	2011–

INDEX OF AUTHORS

INDEX OF FIRST LINES